THE
FEVER

WALLACE SHAWN

The Noonday Press

Farrar, Straus and Giroux

New York

Published simultaneously in Canada by HarperCollinsCanadaLtd
Published simultaneously in hardcover by Farrar, Straus and Giroux
Printed in the United States of America
First printing, 1991
Library of Congress Cataloging-in-Publication Data
Shawn, Wallace.
The fever / Wallace Shawn.
I. Title.
PS3569.H387F48   1991   812'.54—dc20   90-44050
CIP

All inquiries concerning The Fever
should be addressed to Howard Rosenstone,
Rosenstone/Wender, 3 East 48th Street,
New York, New York, 10017.

Also by Wallace Shawn

AUNT DAN AND LEMON

MARIE AND BRUCE

MY DINNER WITH ANDRÉ
(with André Gregory)

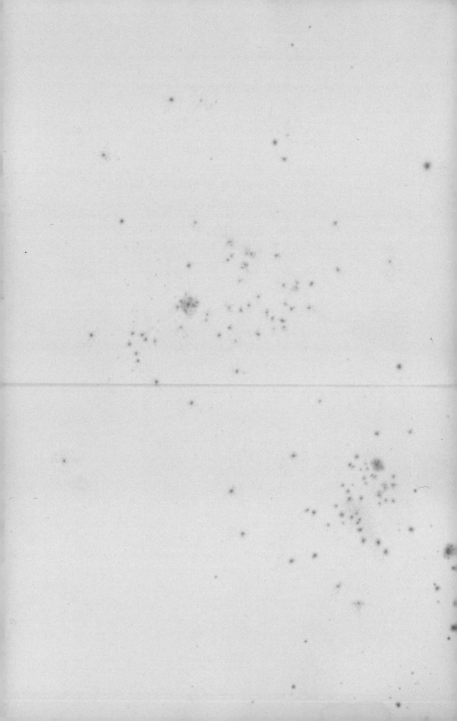

D and W

Julio and Barbara

Deborah and Baltazar

Tom and Christine

The Fever

I'M TRAVELING—and I wake up suddenly in the silence before dawn in a strange hotel room, in a poor country where my language isn't spoken, and I'm shaking and shivering.— Why? There's something—something is happening—far away, in a different country. Yes, I remember. It's the execution. The newspaper article said this would be the hour, this was the date.

I catch my breath. And so now they come— they come for the man who lies on his cot, the cat-like man whose face is so large, so black, that the guards who open his cell are once again frightened, shaken. They shave his head, a section of his leg, so the electrodes will fit closely on the skin.

And now the guards lead him into the chamber, and he's tied into the chair with leather straps. His arms are strapped down to armrests so the witnesses won't see them move, his legs strapped to the legs of the chair— Does panic mount in the man's heart? An attendant covers his head with a hood so none of us will see his pain, the horror, the distortion of his face. The breaking of the skin! All we see is the body shifting upwards, slightly in the chair.

Don't you think—when you're traveling in a strange country—that the smells are sharp and upsetting? And when you wake up in the middle of the night—unexpectedly—when you wake up at an odd hour—when you're traveling somewhere and you wake up in a strange place—don't you feel frightened?

I can't stop shivering.

The lamp by my bed doesn't work, the electric lights won't turn on. The rebels have blown up the electricity towers. There's a small war going on in this poor country where my language isn't spoken. The hotel rooms all have candles with

The Fever

little candle holders. I get up, light the candle, take the candle into the bathroom. Then I put the candle in its holder on the floor, and I kneel down in front of the toilet and vomit.— Then I'm sitting, shivering, on the bathroom floor, this cold square of tile on a hot night in a hot country, and I can't stand up to go back to bed—I can't stand up—so I sit there quietly, shaking as if I were sitting in the snow. And in the corner of the bathroom—brown against the tile—there's an insect, big, like a water bug—it's flat, heavy—very tough legs, they look like metal—and it's waiting, squatting, deciding which way to move.— And in a second it's crossed behind the sink, and it's slipping itself into a hole too small for it to fit in, but it fits—in—it fits—it's gone. And I see myself. I see myself. A moment of insight.

It's the birthday party in the fancy restaurant. Yes—there's the table with its sweet and pretty decorations, the fanciful centerpiece, pink and green, and there are all the women in bright red lipstick and the men in beautiful shirts, and all the gifts—outrageous, unexpected, and funny gifts—and there are the waiters serving the salmon and pouring the wine, and there I am. I'm talking quietly with that small, pale woman in the red-and-blue dress about the love affair with the older man, that film that disturbed her, the actress, the psychiatrist, the criminals, the walks at night through the woods in the country, the insatiable appetite for violent sex, the suffering of the people who live in desperation in the crowded shelter across the street from the fancy restaurant. And as I talked with that woman in the red-and-blue dress, I thought I was a person who was thinking about a party, who had so many complicated feelings about it, who liked some aspects of the party, but not others, who liked some of the people, but not all of them, who liked the pink-and-green centerpiece, but didn't really like that red-and-blue dress. But no. No. I see it so clearly. I see myself with my little fork— I wasn't a person who was thinking about a party. I was a person who was *at* a party, who sat at the table, drank the wine, and ate the fish.

We didn't talk about the fish, we didn't talk about the restaurant, we talked about the lakes in the mountains in the north of Thailand and the crowded shelter across the street. But where were we? Where were we? Not by the lakes, not in the

The Fever

shelter— We were there, just there, at that table, in that restaurant.— Well, maybe for certain people—maybe for certain people who lived at the beginning of the twentieth century—what was hidden and unconscious was the inner life. Maybe the only thing those people could see was the outward circumstance, where they were, what they did, and they had no idea at all of what was inside them. But something's been hidden from me, too. Something—a part of myself—has been hidden from me, and I think it's the part that's there on the surface, what anyone in the world could see about me if they saw me out the window of a passing train.

Because I know quite a bit about what's inside me. I've been a student of my feelings since I was nine years old! My feelings! My thoughts! The incredible history of my feelings and my thoughts could fill up a dozen leather-bound books. But the story of my life—my behavior, my actions— that's a slim volume, and I've never read it. Well, I've never wanted to. I've always thought it would be terribly boring. What would be in it? Chapter One: My Childhood. I was born, I cried. Chapter Two: The Rest: I maintained myself. I got up, I went to work, I went home, I went to bed. I went to a restaurant, and I ate fish. Who cares? For God's sake—did I have to travel to a poor country where no books are printed in my own language —did I have to be cast down onto a bathroom floor in a strange hotel—in order to finally be forced to open that dull volume, the story of my life?

And I vomit again. Dear God.

No, I'm not going to read it. I won't read it. My parents loved me. They raised me to think about people, the world, humanity, beauty—not to think about restaurants and fish. I was born into the mind. Lamplight. The warm living room. My father, in an armchair, reading about China. My mother with the newspaper on a long sofa. Orange juice on a table in a glass pitcher.

And they read me a book about all the people in so many different uniforms who came to our house to help our family: coming from every corner of our beautiful city, the delivery man from the grocery store, the mailman with the mail. All so kind. And down the street, the old woman who worked in the bakery, who bent down and gave me sugar-covered buns. And, dear God, I never

The Fever

doubtcd that life was precious. I've always thought life should be *celebrated*.

Today, I went to an office, a quiet office—a few cabinets and chairs—and its job was to make a record of all the cases of political murder, and torture, and rape—rape used as a form of torture or in the course of torture. There were photographs on the walls of the bleeding corpses of friends. The blood was bright red. One was a schoolteacher, killed near her school. And there were black-and-white snapshots of shyly smiling women and men at some time before their deaths, and these were pinned up next to the pictures of their corpses. The faces, radiant with goodness.

And I thought of the delicacy with which my parents had taught me to urinate into the toilet, to be careful around toilet seats, to wash my hands, always with soap, to avoid people with the flu, with colds, to avoid drafts, to avoid rooms that were cold or wet.

And I thought of how they'd taught me to love traveling—the wonderful train trips. The magic of riding at night through the farmland in our little compartment, brushing our teeth on the moving train.

And here, from my spot on the bathroom floor, I can see through the window, gorgeous in the moonlight, the gorgeous mountains of the poor country, soaked with the blood of the innocent, soaked with the blood of those shy faces, battered shy faces.

Walking through a garden with my mother— enormous roses. And through a dark pine forest— my father pointing to a yellow bird. Save me.

You see, *I* like Beethoven. *I* like to hear the bow of the violin *cut* into the string. *I* like to follow the phrase of the violin as it goes on and on, like a deep-rooted orgasm squeezed out into a rope of sound. *I* like to go out at night in a cosmopolitan city and sit in a dark auditorium watching dancers fly into each other's arms.

Yes, suppose that certain people—certain people whose hearts admittedly are filled with love— *are* being awakened suddenly at night by groups of armed men. Suppose that they *are* being dragged into a stinking van with a carpet on the floor and stomped by boots till their lips are swollen like oranges, streaming with blood. Yes, I was alive when those things were done, I lived in the town whose streets ran with the blood of good-

The Fever

hearted victims, I wore the clothes which were pulled from the bodies of the victims when they were raped and killed.

But I love the violin. I love the music, the dancers, everything I touch, everything I see. The city with its lights, the theaters, coffeeshops, newsstands, books. The constant celebration. Life should be celebrated. Life is a gift.

And I can't stand the way people say, "When I was a child, I loved elephants," "When I was a child, I loved balloons." Are they trying to say that if they stopped and looked at a balloon today or at an elephant today, they would *not* love them? Why *wouldn't* they love them? I think we still love what we always loved. How could we not? And one of the things that *I* always loved—I wonder if you did—was the wonderful way that valuable small objects—the Christmas presents and birthday presents that adults always gave to each other—were wrapped, were packed. Say the present was a small china cup or saucer or a tiny china vase. Well, first there'd be a brown cardboard box from the shop that looked like it ought to have a rocking horse or tricycle inside, because it was just so big—except that, if you lifted it, it was always incredibly, miraculously light—and you would always imagine that that big brown box had been packed up and sealed up by some sort of huge and muscle-y industrial workers who were completely indifferent to the contents of the box. And then someone would make a cut with a knife in the brown tape at the top of the box, and when they pulled the two halves of the top apart, there would always be a huge sort of industrial snapping sound. And then inside that big cardboard box you'd find another box, wrapped in thick shiny paper and tied with some brightly colored thick shiny ribbon, which wasn't really needed to keep the box closed, and you would naturally imagine that this inside box had been wrapped by some very refined and modest-looking lady whose hands were softened with sweet-smelling cream and who very definitely cared a great deal about whatever it was that was inside the box. And then when the paper and the ribbon were undone and removed, and the box itself, with its smooth surface like clear milk, was finally revealed, someone would take off the top of the box, and you would hear at that moment a little rustling or nestling sound, like the sound of a hamster moving in its cage, and that would

The Fever

be the sound of all the tiny little pieces of
squunched-up paper that filled the box giving a
sort of quiet little sigh as the taking off of the top
of the box gave them some sudden extra breathing
space. And then the most exciting part of the
opening would start, which was the attempt to
find out what in particular was inside the box *aside*
from all the pieces of squunched-up paper, if in
fact there was anything else inside there at all,
because at first you always thought, Well, really,
this time there *is* nothing else. So then someone—
maybe you—would plunge their hand down deep
into the box as if they were a diver searching for
a pearl, and eventually they would come upon
something hard, something tightly wrapped in a
different sort of paper, and when that last bit of
wrapping was finally undone, there would be the
cup or saucer or tiny little vase, just suitable for
one little flower. And maybe if you'd seen that
cup or saucer or vase just sitting on a shelf in a
shop somewhere, you might have thought it was
nothing in particular, or maybe if you'd seen it
lying in a pile with heaps of others like it in the
corner of some dark dusty place that sold odds
and ends, you would have thought it was an old

piece of junk, but by the time it had been pulled out of all that paper, out of that milk-white box, out of that cardboard carton, it seemed like the most shining, sparkling thing in the world. And how delicate it seemed—how breakable and precious. And you were right, it was.

And my friends and I were the delicate, precious, breakable children, and we always knew it. We knew it because of the way we were wrapped—because of the soft underwear laid out on our beds, soft socks to protect our feet.

And I remember that my darling mother, my beautiful mother, my innocent mother would say to me and my friends, when we were nine or ten, "Now be very careful, don't go near First Avenue. That's a bad neighborhood. There are tough kids there."

And we had no idea what that meant. She had no idea. We thought that certain kids were tough—maybe they just liked to be. And they lived in certain neighborhoods—maybe because their friends were there. Nice people had gathered in our neighborhood, had formed a community, and it was a good neighborhood. On First Avenue and other avenues, there were bad neighborhoods,

The Fever

where tough people had gathered together, and those were the neighborhoods we had to avoid.

We still avoid them—all of my friends. Bad neighborhoods. The people who live in places like that would hurt you, beat you, cut you, kill you. All the ones who would hurt you collect in those neighborhoods, like water in drains. And it's terrible. It's awful. Why should people want to hurt each other? I always say to my friends, We should be glad to be alive. We should celebrate life. We should understand that life is wonderful.

Shouldn't we decorate our lives and our world as if we were having a permanent party? Shouldn't there be bells made of paper hanging from the ceiling, and paper balls, and white and yellow streamers? Shouldn't people dance and hold each other close? Shouldn't we fill the tables with cake and presents?

Yes, but we can't have celebrations in the very same room where groups of people are being tortured, or groups of people are being killed. We have to know, Where are we, and where are the ones who are being tortured and killed? Not in the same room? No—but surely—isn't there any other room we can use? Yes, but we still could hear the people screaming. Well, then—can't we use the building across the street? Well, maybe—but wouldn't it feel strange to walk by the window during our celebrations and look across at the building we're in now and think about the blood and the deaths and the testicles being crushed inside it?

Who are the ones who are being tortured and killed? It was explained to me: the followers of Marx.

The dizziness drops my head to the floor. I feel as if a rope that's been wrapped around my temples is being tightened and released, tightened and released, and there's an aching pain in the center of my stomach.

In my own country I've always loved staying in hotels. In fact, one of the things I think I like best is to sleep in a hotel in some new city and then to get up early while the birds are singing and call room service and get them to send me up a big pot of coffee, and then to lie in bed and call my friends on the telephone while I sip my coffee. I can spend literally hours like that, just talking on the telephone and laughing and drinking more coffee and watching the sun coming in the win-

The Fever

dow and moving around the room. And then I get up and go about my day.

But staying in a hotel in a foreign country is always different.

I'll tell you about a funny incident that happened at lunch today. Well, it was my own reaction that was funny, really. The hotel had a banquet. Everyone had huge plates of food: pork, shrimp, lobster, game. I stood outside, and there was a girl of maybe sixteen who sat on some steps not far from me. She was a peasant girl, barefoot, her legs peeping out from a faded skirt. Her eyes were blurred, as if she'd been whipped. She was waiting for something, carved into the corner of the stone steps in an attitude of incredible gravity and grace. Suddenly, a young man with a foolish expression came out of the hotel, dressed in a suit. He was heading toward the girl on the steps, and from the way he waved at her I realized she must have been one of his family's maids. He was holding out to her a tiny little plate with a few beans on it. That was her lunch. Well, she smiled to acknowledge that gift of food, and I had an immediate reaction—I wanted to punch that young man in the face, throw him in the bushes. It was really quite funny. What did I think I was, this week's radical guerrilla? Then he went back inside—oblivious of me, of course—and the moment passed.

About a year ago I spent a day at a nude beach with a group of people I didn't know that well. Lying out there, naked, in the sun, there was a man who kept talking about "the ruling class," "the elite," "the rich." All day long, "The rich are pigs, they are *all* pigs, some day those pigs will get what they deserve," and things like that. He was a thin man with a large mustache, unhealthy-looking but very handsome, a chain-smoker. As he talked, he would laugh—sort of bitter barks that came out always unexpectedly. I'd heard about these words and these phrases all of my life, but I'd never met anyone who actually used them. I thought it was quite entertaining. But for about a month afterward a strange thing happened. Everywhere I went I started getting into conversations with people I met—on a train, on a bus, at parties, in the line for a movie—and everyone I met was talking like him: The rich are pigs, their day will come, they're all pigs, and on and on. I started to think that maybe I was crazy. I thought

The Fever

I was insane. Could this really be happening? Was everyone now a Communist but me?

And this was all happening at the very same time that Communism had finally died, and social pathologists were arguing over what had caused its death. The newspapers and magazines reported no nostalgia for the defunct system, and it seemed as if all the intellectuals and political leaders who had ever been known to have fallen under its sway were running in all directions looking for shelter. So then who were all these people who kept grabbing hold of me?

One day there was an anonymous present sitting on my doorstep—Volume One of *Capital* by Karl Marx, in a brown paper bag. A joke? Serious? And who had sent it? I never found out. Late that night, naked in bed, I leafed through it. The beginning was impenetrable, I couldn't understand it, but when I came to the part about the lives of the workers—the coal miners, the child laborers— I could feel myself suddenly breathing more slowly. How angry he was. Page after page. Then I turned back to an earlier section, and I came to a phrase that I'd heard before, a strange, upsetting, sort of ugly phrase: this was the section on "commodity fetishism," "the fetishism of commodities." I wanted to understand that weird-sounding phrase, but I could tell that, to understand it, your whole life would probably have to change.

His explanation was very elusive. He used the example that people say, "Twenty yards of linen are worth two pounds." People say about every thing that it has a certain value. This is worth that. This coat, this sweater, this cup of coffee: each thing worth some quantity of money, or some number of other things—one coat, worth three sweaters, or so much money—as if that coat, suddenly appearing on the earth, contained somewhere inside itself an amount of value, like an inner soul, as if the coat were a fetish, a physical object that contains a living spirit. But what really determines the value of a coat? What is it that determines the price of a coat? The coat's price comes from its history, the history of all the people who were involved in making it and selling it and all the particular relationships they had. And if we buy the coat, we, too, form relationships with all of those people, and yet we hide those relationships from our own awareness by pretending we live in a world where coats have no history

The Fever

but just fall down from heaven with prices marked inside. "I like this coat," we say, "It's not expensive," as if that were a fact about the *coat* and not the end of a story about all the people who made it and sold it, "I like the pictures in this magazine."

A naked woman leans over a fence. A man buys a magazine and stares at her picture. The destinies of these two are linked. The man has paid the woman to take off her clothes, to lean over the fence. The photograph contains its history—the moment the woman unbuttoned her shirt, how she felt, what the photographer said. The price of the magazine is a code that describes the relationships between all those people—the woman, the man, the publisher, the photographer—who commanded, who obeyed. The cup of coffee contains the history of the peasants who picked the beans, how some of them fainted in the heat of the sun, some were beaten, some were kicked.

For two days I could see the fetishism of commodities everywhere around me. It was a strange feeling. Then on the third day I lost it, it was gone, I couldn't see it anymore.

But, not long after the gift of the book, I was waiting for a bus. Someone with a very nice smile was standing behind me, their thin chest covered by a faded T-shirt, and written on the T-shirt was a single word: it was the name of a revolutionary country. The bus was delayed, it got later and later, and I finally smiled at the smile that was standing behind me, and I asked the person, "Have you been to that country—the one on your shirt?" And the person said, "Yes—have you been there, too?" with a flush of warmth coming into their face. Then a bus pulled up, and the person got on, but it wasn't my bus.

About six months later I'd been to a party in an elegant part of town, and I'd had a lot to drink. It was a dark night. The streets were wet. I was racing along by some blue trees, and suddenly I saw a pool of light, and in the center of the light a walnut-faced man with gray hair in a dusky suit was hailing a taxi. He'd been at the party, but we hadn't spoken. He asked me if I was going his way, and I was. His accent was musical. We got in the taxi. His hands were shaking with an odd tremor, and his voice sounded like a thick dark syrup. He was speaking in these very condensed

The Fever

and ironic phrases, and after a while I awkwardly said, "I can't place your accent—where are you from?" He looked at me darkly and with particular irony he revealed that he came from the revolutionary country whose name I had seen on the T-shirt months before. He worked for that country as a diplomat. "Is it difficult to travel to your country?" I asked. He explained mildly that you could find yourself there in a matter of hours.

A few months later I went to the revolutionary country. It wasn't like the lies I'd heard about it. There were lots of soldiers, that was a fact, but to me they looked more like shepherds in Renaissance paintings. Their green uniforms looked like pajamas. I was very refreshed. I talked to officials who got to their offices at dawn—they were all very tired, but very polite, gentle, humorous—some were very warm, some seemed wistful. One day I stopped in a public square, and I wrote in my notebook the romantic sentence: "These shy smiles are like a garden for me." I stayed in an eccentric expensive hotel, and the ice cream there seemed to me like a drug—delicious, perfect, light and aromatic. I couldn't get enough of this amazing ice cream. A journalist I met who was staying at the hotel explained to me that it didn't make sense to admire a revolution because of its ice cream, because it could really be considered an *imperfection* in the revolution that resources would be devoted to making ice cream at all when some people still didn't have enough to eat. His remark was valid, but he missed the point: the ice cream was charming.

I continued my trip, and I decided to go to more poor countries. I went to poor countries whose names were written on no T-shirts, where the soldiers had strange expressions on their faces, where wealthy families sat in glittering restaurants eating plate after plate of multicolored ice cream, but when I tasted the ice cream, every flavor tasted the same, and none were delicious. I grew weak hearing descriptions of electrical torture, the condition of bodies. I saw orchards of unsurpassed beauty where workers had been raped and hung from the trees. But one bright sunny Sunday I went to a tiny church, crowded with gaunt faces, and there was joyful singing, and the priest spoke of a loving Christ, the importance of forgiveness—tolerance, mercy. And one afternoon in a dark café I drank a cup of tea with an armed guerrilla.

The Fever

Juana, a follower of Marx. It was a little bit scary. Her skin was yellowish, her eyes too bright. She seemed to be on fire with a painful illness. Well, not really a follower of Marx. But his name seemed wonderful to her, even his picture seemed beautiful, because unlike the other philosophers and the educated people, she explained to me, Marx had made the strange gesture of throwing his life at the feet of the poor. In other words, *Marx* was a follower of *theirs*. He was on their side.

I kept trying to get her to talk about herself. She hadn't seen her home for a long time. She loved her parents. She had two small children. Her husband had died in his early twenties. She spoke to me feverishly about a sister who'd been killed, clenching and unclenching her hands. Her sister's head had been mutilated. After her sister's death, she'd left her village and walked into the mountains to find the rebels. She'd learned how to go without eating for days. The poise, the dignity, of a wild animal.

I went home, and I resumed my regular life. But I couldn't help noticing that something awful was happening to me. At first I tried to ignore it or dismiss it, like some symptom you hope will go away by itself, but it didn't go away. What was it that was happening? I'd always said, "I'm a happy person. I love life," but now there was a sort of awful indifference or blankness that was coming from somewhere inside me and filling me up, bit by bit. Things that would once have delighted me or cheered me seemed to go dead on me, to spoil. Sometimes it was as if someone was strangling me.

I went to see some people I knew—close friends. I'd never visited their home before, and we'd all been looking forward to my visit for years. "This is our bedroom," opening a door. "The baby sleeps here." Each room was beautiful— each had a simple tastefulness, there were striking touches, there were lovely objects from around the world. In the children's rooms there was blue-sky wallpaper even on the ceiling, shelves with big yellow chickens and ducks. But I felt wrong. I felt sick. I felt nothing—a numbness.

I went to a play with a group of friends—a legendary actress in a great role. We stared at the stage. Moment after moment the character's downfall crept closer. Her childhood home would

The Fever

at last be sold, her beloved cherry trees chopped down. Under the bright lights, the actress showed anger, bravado, the stage rang with her youthful laughter, which expressed self-deception. She would be forced to live in an apartment in Paris, not on the estate she'd formerly owned. Her former serf would buy the estate. It was her old brother's sympathetic grief that finally coaxed tears from the large man in the heavy coat who sat beside me. But my problem was that somehow, suddenly, I was not myself. I was disconcerted. Why, exactly, were we supposed to be weeping? This person would no longer own the estate she'd once owned . . . She would have to live in an apartment instead . . . I couldn't remember why I was supposed to be weeping.

Riding in a taxi home from the play, my friends were critical of one of the actors. His performance had been slack, inadequate, not thought through. If the character he played behaved in such a fashion in the First Act, his later actions could not be explained. I stared, frozen, out the taxi window.

Sometimes I was fine. I remember one morning—a marvelous blue sky—I had my hair cut.

Gentle hands molded my hair so it fit over the shape of my scalp like a cap. Then I bought myself a pair of comfortable socks, and then I looked at them carefully, and I bought two more pairs, because it's not easy to find the kind of socks I like! Then I went to a sweet little restaurant and had lunch with a woman in a lemon-yellow suit whom I'd known since I was eight. But then I got into a taxi, and as I was riding across the city, that feeling, that sickness, filled me up again. It seemed to start in my stomach and move out through my legs, my chest. And my stomach was beating, it was just like a heart. A cold sweat on my forehead and neck. I wasn't me. When the taxi arrived, the person who got out of it wasn't me. *I* was nowhere. The person who paid the driver was actually no one.

Someone with whom I'd had a very happy love affair years ago was waiting to meet me. We smiled, we embraced, but I wasn't there to be embraced. The person I was hugging felt like a doll, electrically warmed. I myself was a funny-smelling doll. In the old apartment, full of memories, we talked about a recent play, a film, a terrible performance by a group of dancers, one

The Fever

of whom we knew, and I heard about the dinner
with our friend Nadia, who was working on her
painting but also was doing graphic design, and
the story of the wooden figures smuggled out of
Mexico wrapped in clothes. Our funny friend
Petrus had had his wallet stolen. Amazingly, the
police had caught the thief as he was running
down the street. Petrus had said the man's crim-
inal record was as long as that biography of Henry
James. The adventures of Petrus with the police
and the courts were a hilarious comedy, Petrus
being Petrus. But as I listened to the story, I re-
membered that a friend of my mother's had once
said to me, "I like you, because you have such a
nice, loud, merry laugh," and I noticed that my
laugh was like a tight little cough.

We were going to have dinner with another
friend of ours in a hotel dining room near the
office where he worked, but when we met our
friend, we wandered by mistake into the hotel
ballroom. There were prosperous-looking executives, probably retired, dancing with their wives
to awful music—men with baggy pants and big
thighs and coins in their pockets—and their wives
were wearing flowery dresses, with their hair like

wigs, and our friend said, "God, how unhappy they are. How painful it is. How sad life is," but I stared at the executives in their dark suits and felt only that numbness, it was even in my mouth, on my tongue, a sort of sour lovelessness, a sort of horrible rotting lovelessness.

And toward the end of dinner our friend finally told us that his father had died. He described the hospital, the doctors, the machines. It was as if he felt no one had ever died before, as if he felt it was quite unfair that his father should have died. Yet no expense had been spared to extend his father's life for as long as possible, to make sure that his death was as comfortable as possible. Hardworking experts surrounded his bed doing all they could to see that he would die without feeling pain. I couldn't help mentioning those others who died every day on the torture table, screaming, carved up with knives, surrounded on *their* bed of death by *other* experts who were doing all *they* could to be sure that the ones *they* surrounded would die in howling agony—unimaginable agony.

My remarks were out of place. Where was the

The Fever

sympathy I owed my friend? His loss was real. He looked at me, appalled.

By then it was Christmas. A festive atmosphere filled the streets and shops, and one night I had a dream, and I dreamt it was Christmas, and I had a wonderful family, with two or three young children, and in the dream I woke up suddenly, frightened and sweating, and I went to the bathroom to brush my teeth. My toothbrush, paste, and water glass were crowded as usual onto a shelf. As I glanced into the bathroom mirror for a moment, the shelf on which all these things rested started to tilt. My water glass slid slowly along it, then fell and broke on the tile into thick, sharp pieces. I lost my balance, slipped, and stepped directly onto a shard of glass. Blood filled the floor. My family came. I was crying, sobbing. "I'm sorry," I said, "I cannot give you any more presents. I love you all, but I don't want to give you any more presents." The words came flying out of my mouth. I didn't know why I was saying them. I'd always wanted my children to be happy. I'd always wanted them to have the best of everything. Then I woke up and thought about the dream, the presents. I thought about Christmas, the streets, the shops. Was that why people brought children into the world—so that they, too, could one day roam through the streets, buying, devouring, always "the best"—the best food, the best clothes, the best everything—so that they, too, could demand "the best"? Were there not enough people in the world already who demanded the best, who insisted on the best? No, we must bring in more, and then we must gather together more treasures from all over the world, more of the best, for all these new children of ours to have, because our children should have the best, it would be our shame, our disgrace, to give them less than the best. We will stop at nothing to give them the best.

I was in a very bad state. And it wasn't that I'd particularly loved the trip I'd just taken. But I felt that maybe I should go back again—go back again to more poor countries—that maybe that was the thing I should do to cure my feeling of sickness or restlessness, or whatever it was. I even had a suitcase that was still not unpacked. And so I thought—Well—maybe—and here I am.

My last night in my own country I spent in an

The Fever

airport hotel. The people in the room above mine were playing music much too late. I called the front desk and complained. As I lay in bed, I imagined the people above me listening. They were dressed in comfortable, informal clothes—they were free, happy, maybe a little bit drunk or high. Maybe they were dancing. I'd always been so fond of the song they were playing—a beautiful song—and I felt a sort of exquisite pleasure: lying against my pillow, listening to the song, waiting for the moment when the hotel detective would knock on the door of the room above mine and the music would suddenly stop in mid-phrase.

I try to stand up to leave the bathroom. I get to my knees, but I can't stand up. Draped over the bathtub there's a purple bath mat. I grab it, I pull it onto the floor, I pull it over toward me, and I slide it beneath me.

Do you know!—there are nights in the city where I grew up, the city I love most of all, when it's too cold for rain, but the sky can't snow yet, although you feel it would like to, and so instead it seems that at a certain moment every car and face and pane of glass is suddenly covered by a delicious wetness, like the wetness you see on a frozen cherry, and on nights like that, when you walk through the streets of the nice parts of town, you see all the men, in overcoats that hang straight down to the ground, staring harshly with open-mouthed desire at the fox-headed women whose lipstick ripples, whose earrings ripple, as they step through the uneven light and darkness of the sidewalk. And that is the sort of thing that the Communists will never understand. That is the sort of thing that the Communists will never understand, just as human decency is the sort of thing that I will never understand.

Look—here's a question I'd like to ask you—Have you ever had any friends who were poor? See, I think that's an idea a lot of people have: "Why shouldn't I have some friends who are poor?"

I've pictured it so often, like a dream that comes again and again. There've been so many people—people who work at menial jobs whom I've seen every day—people who've caught my eye, talked to me, and I've thought, How nice, It's nice, If only—and I've imagined it—but then what I imagine always ends so badly.

The Fever

I always picture that they invite you to come over to their home for dinner, and—I don't know what it is—it's something about the light bulbs, the flooring that's coming up just a tiny little bit from the floor, and you walk in and you say to yourself, It's fine, this is fine, it's all just fine, but you know it isn't—and there's a sort of sticky smell coming from somewhere, from a hallway, a room, and the television, and the walls are painted with this kind of shiny pink, and there are children who are sick and sneezing and coughing. And there are some hard chairs, and you end up sitting on the floor, and you're squirming around on the floor, and you're trying to find some support for your back. And they give you some food, and the meat is greasy, and the piece of meat seems to get bigger and bigger as it sits on your plate. And everyone's being incredibly nice. And somebody changes the baby's diaper. And then a week later they call and invite you again, and you don't know what to say, so you go once again, and then once again maybe a few months later, and then—I don't know—maybe you move to another part of town, maybe you move out of town altogether, maybe *they* move out of town—but the next time you go is a year later, and then there never is a time after that.

Dear God, what's happening to me? I feel like there's nothing left of me. I feel like I don't think anything—I don't remember— . . . What are the things I always say? I believe that there are— . . . I believe that—

No—now stop that. Every person is a person, every person believes certain things. My friend Bob—my friend Bob believes that "democracy is the worst form of government, except for all the others." And Fred—Fred believes that "today's rebel is tomorrow's dictator." And Natasha believes that peasants in poor countries just want to be left alone to farm their fields in peace and quiet, and they couldn't care less about the ideologies of the right or the left. Mario believes that social criticism in plays and films can be expressed most effectively through the use of humor. And Indrani believes that works of art, including performances of opera and ballet, can change individuals and, through them, society. And Toshiko believes that the only real contribution that people can make toward solving the problems of the world is to raise their own families with good values. And Ann-Marie believes that the rich and the poor should live as friends and should work together to make the future better than the past.

But the question—the question is—Would it really matter if it were *Fred* who believed that democracy is the worst form of government, except for all the others? What if Fred were to wake up one morning and *think* he believed that, forgetting that that was actually the belief of his friend Bob?

Fred believes certain things—you can say that. But what does it mean? Does it mean something? I don't remember . . . —

And my beliefs? Yes, yes—I have beliefs, yes—I believe in humanity, sympathy for others—I oppose cruelty and violence—

What? You applaud cruelty and violence?

No—I said I oppose cruelty and violence—Jesus Christ—oppose, oppose—

But I can still remember what I like—can't I?—if not what I believe. I know what I like. I like warmth, coziness, pleasure, love—mail, pres-

ents—nice plates—those paintings by Matisse . . .
Yes, I'm an aesthete. I like beauty.

Yes—poor countries are beautiful. Poor people
are beautiful. It's a wonderful feeling to have
money in a country where most people are poor,
to ride in a taxi through horrible slums.

Yes—a beggar can be beautiful. A beggar can
have beautiful lips, beautiful eyes. You're far from
home. To you, her simple shawl seems elegant,
direct, the right way to dress. You see her ap-
proaching from a great distance. She's old, thin,
and yes, she looks sick, very sick, near death. But
her face is beautiful—seductive, luminous. You
like her—you're drawn to her. Yes, you think—
there's money in your purse—you'll give her some
of it.

And a voice says—Why not all of it? Why not
give her all that you have?

Be careful, that's a question that could poison
your life. Your love of beauty could actually kill
you.

If you hear that question, it means you're
sick. You're mentally sick. You've had a break-
down.

And the bathroom spins, all the way around,

at a sort of unbearable speed. I stare at the toilet.

Answer the question, idiot. Don't just stand there. I can't give the beggar all that I have, because I—

because I—

be—

Wait a minute. Wait a minute. I *have* beliefs. There's a *reason* why I won't give the beggar all of my money. Yes, I'm going to give her *some* of it—I always give away quite a surprising amount to people who have less than I do— But there's a reason why *I'm* the one who *has* the money in the *first* place, and *that's* why I'm not going to give it all away. In other words, for God's sake, I *worked* for that money. I worked hard. I worked. I worked. I worked hard to make that money, and it's my money, because I made it. *I* made the money, and so *I* have it, and *I* can spend it any way I like. This is the basis of our entire lives. Why can I stay here in this hotel? Because I paid to stay here, with my money. I paid to stay here, and that entitles me to certain things. I'm entitled to stay here, I'm entitled to be served, I'm entitled to expect that certain things will be done. Now, this morning, for example, the chambermaid left my room a mess. The floor was dirty, there were no clean sheets, and the wastepaper basket was left full. So I paid to stay here, I paid to be served, I'm entitled to service, but the chambermaid didn't serve me properly. That was wrong.

And I'm seized by another fit of vomiting. My shoulders reach forward toward the toilet and pull me with them. My head drives toward the bowl of the toilet, and I vomit again and again and again.

Why is the old woman sick and dying? Why doesn't she have money? Didn't she ever work?

You idiot, you pathetic idiot, of course she worked. She worked sixteen hours a day in a field, in a factory. She worked, the chambermaid worked.— You say *you* work. But why does your work bring you so much money, while their work brings practically nothing? You say you "make" money. What a wonderful expression. But how can you "make" so much of it in such a short time, while in the same amount of time they "make" so little?

Heat runs all over me in little waves, and the purple of my bath mat gets deeper and deeper, and enormous, fat water bugs cover the floor,

The Fever

running, fast. Hundreds of them, running in patterns. I stand up to avoid them, and a tall revolutionary guard in an undershirt is lifting his foot. He's lifting his foot. And then he twirls around, and he kicks me in the face, and I fall backward, and I land on a bunk, a hard bunk. And I'm in a cell, and the guard reaches into a big bag, and he pulls out this slim little book, and it's vaguely familiar. And then he throws it at me and leaves the cell. "Read it," he says. "Read it. Read it."

I run to the door of the cell and I scream—Is this what you call the power of the people?—but he's gone away. I scream and scream till my throat aches. But now I'm alone with the ugly little book. My hands drip with sweat as I sit on the bunk and start to read.

Sure, it's just exactly what I expected it to be. The most tedious questions, answered in full, as if a person's life were a customs form. Chapter One: What country I grew up in, what city, what street? My parents' race. The money they made. What I was fed. What I was taught. Chapter Two: This is unbelievable—printed in the book: "Washes hair every day unless 'in a hurry'" quote unquote; "when meeting friends for dinner or going to the theater, takes a bath in the late afternoon, puts on fresh clothes." What in the world is going on? This has absolutely nothing to do with what *I* am like, with anything at all that's important about me! Don't they know that everything in this book is just as true of—of—of my neighbor Jean as it is of me, my neighbor Jean who makes jokes about starving children in Asia, my neighbor Jean who boasts about fucking colleagues at the office on the boardroom table? Don't they know that?

One of the guards holds my arms behind my back, the other one starts hitting me in the face with his fists. He hits me in the face several times, then in the chest, and then in the stomach. No one in my life has ever hit me before. I'm thinking about the damage each blow might do. And a little bit of blood is coming out of my mouth.

Then there's another guard, a woman whose face is like a cake that's been soaked in rage. She's standing to the side, and my cries are echoing in the cell—"No! No!" And then she comes up to me, and she spits in my face. And I'm screaming out at her, "For God's sake, what have I done to

make you feel like this? What in the world have
I done to you?"

When the guards leave, I cry like an animal. I
can't stop thinking about my mother—the way
she took care of me—I can't stand this.

I control myself, get a grip on myself. I have
to survive. And so I sit on my bunk and cry and
read and cry and read. And time passes—so much
time—it seems like forever—and then yes, yes, I
understand—I see that there's an answer to the
question I asked. Yes, it could have been pre-
dicted, from knowing these things—where I was
born, how I was raised—what an hour of my labor
would probably be worth—even though, to me,
from the inside, my life always felt like a story
that was just unfolding, unpredictable. Yes, I was
born, and a field was provided, a piece of land,
from which rich fruit could be plucked by eager
hands. And I was taught to be very eager. The
beggar, the chambermaid—of course—if you
knew—their childhood villages—no, they weren't
taught to be eager— Here is your land, your piece
of land—it was barren, black, uncultivable.

And I see the whole world laid out like a map

in four dimensions—all the land, the people, the moments of time—today, yesterday. And at each particular moment I can see that the world has a certain very particular ability to produce the things that people need: there's a certain quantity of land that's ready to be farmed, a certain particular number of workers, a certain stock of machinery, a stock of ideas about how to do things, how to organize all the ones who will work. And each day's capacity seems somehow so small. It's fixed, determinate. Every part of it is fixed. And I can see all the days that have happened already, and on each one of them, a determinate number of people worked, and a determinate portion of all the earth's resources was drawn up and used, and a determinate little pile of goods was produced. So small: across the grid of infinite possibility, this finite capacity, distributed each day.

And of all the things that might have been done, which were the ones that actually happened?

The holders of money determine what's done— they bid their money for the things they want, each one according to the amount they hold— and each bit of money determines some fraction of the day's activities, so those who have a little

The Fever

determine a little, and those who have a lot determine a lot, and those who have nothing determine nothing. And then the world obeys the instructions of the money to the extent of its capacity, and then it stops. It's done what it can. The day is over. Certain things happened. If money was bid for jewelry, there was silver that was bent into the shape of a ring. If it was bid for opera, there were costumes that were sewn and chandeliers that were hung on invisible threads.

And there's an amazing moment: Each day, before the day starts, before the market opens, before the bidding begins, there's a moment of confusion: The money is silent, it hasn't yet spoken. Its decisions are withheld, poised, perched, ready. Everyone knows that the world will not do everything today: if food is produced for the hungry children, then certain operas will not be performed; if certain performances are in fact given, then the food won't be produced, and the children will die.

I pull myself over to the window—it doesn't have bars—and I stick my head out. I like weeping in the warm wind. But I feel the presence of a friend behind me, sitting on my bunk, smoking quietly—and wait—it's that guard! And so I can't help impulsively speaking and saying, Look, I'm a human being! Yes, of course I want to make a good wage—What do you think a human being is? A human being happens to be an unprotected little wriggling creature, a little raw creature without a shell or a hide or even any fur, just thrown out onto the earth like an eye that's been pulled from its socket, like a shucked oyster that's trying to crawl along the ground. We need to build our own shells—yes, shoes, chairs, walls, floors, and for God's sake, yes, a little solace, a little consolation. Because Jesus Christ—*you* know, you *know*, we wanted to be happy, we wanted our lives to be absolutely great. We were looking forward for so long to some wonderful night in some wonderful hotel, some wonderful breakfast set out on a tray—we were looking forward, like panting dogs, slobbering on the rug—how we would delight the ones we loved with our kisses in bed, how we would delight our parents with our great accomplishments, how we would delight our children with toys and surprises. But it was all wrong: it was never really right: the hotel, the breakfast, what happened in bed, our parents, our chil-

The Fever

dren—and so yes, we need solace, we need consolation, we need nice food, we need nice things to wear, we need beautiful paintings, movies, plays, drives in the country, bottles of wine. There's never *enough* solace, never *enough* consolation.

I'm doing whatever I possibly can. I try to be nice. I try to be lighthearted, entertaining, funny. I tell entertaining stories to people. I make jokes to the janitor, every single morning, to the parking-lot attendant, every single morning. I try to be amusing whenever I can be, to help my friends get through the day. I write little notes to people I like when I enjoy the articles they've written or their performances in the theater. When a group of people at a party were making unpleasant comments about advertising men, I steered the conversation to a different topic, because my friend Monica was feeling uncomfortable because her father works as an advertising man.

The bunk is empty, except for the book, but the pages of the book run with blood as I pick it up, soaking my clothes, spilling over the floor. There's still the preface—everything that happened before I was born. The voluptuous field that was given to me—how did I come to be given *that* one, and not the one that was black and barren? Yes, it happened like that because before I was born, the fields were apportioned, and some of the fields were pieced together.

Not by chance, not by fate. The fields were pieced together one by one, by thieves, by killers. Over years, over centuries, night after night, knives glittering, throats cut, again and again, until the beautiful Christmas morning we woke up, and our proud parents showed us the gorgeous, shining, blood-soaked fields which now were ours. Cultivate, they said, husband everything you pull from the earth, guard, save, then give your own children the next hillside, the next valley. From each advantage, draw up more. Grow, cultivate, preserve, guard. Drive forward till you have everything. The others will always fall back, retreat, give you what you want or sell you what you want for the price you want. They have no choice, because they're sick and weak. They've become "the poor."

And the book runs on, years, centuries, till the moment comes when our parents say the time of

The Fever

apportionment is now over. We have what we need—our position well defended from every side. Now, finally, everything can be frozen, just as it is. The violence can stop. From now on, no more stealing, no more killing. From this moment, an eternal silence, the rule of law.

So we have everything, but there's one difficulty we just can't overcome, a curse: we can't escape our connection to the poor.

We need the poor. Without the poor to get the fruit off the trees, to tend the excrement under the ground, to bathe our babies on the day they're born, we couldn't exist. Without the poor to do awful work, we would spend our lives doing awful work. If the poor were not poor, if the poor were paid the way we're paid, we couldn't afford to buy an apple, a shirt, we couldn't afford to take a trip, to spend a night at an inn in a nearby town. But the horror is that the poor grow everywhere, like moss, grass. And we can never forget the time when they owned the land. We can never forget the death of their families, those vows of revenge screamed out in those rooms that were running with gore. And the poor don't forget. They live on their rage. They eat rage. They want to rise up and finish us, wipe us off the earth as soon as they can.

And so in our frozen world, our silent world, we have to talk to the poor. Talk, listen, clarify, explain. They want things to be different. They want change. And so we say, Yes. Change. But not violent change. Not theft, not revolt, not revenge. Instead, listen to the idea of gradual change. Change that will help you, but that won't hurt us. Morality. Law. Gradual change. We explain it all: a two-sided contract: we'll give you things, many things, but in exchange you must accept that you don't have the right just to take what you want. We're going to give you wonderful things. Sit down, wait, don't try to grab— The most important thing is patience, waiting. We're going to give you much much more than you're getting now, but there are certain things that must happen first—these are the things for which we must wait. First, we have to make more and we have to grow more, so more will be available for us to give. Otherwise, if we give you more, we'll have less. When we make more and we grow more, we can all have more—some of the increase can go to

The Fever

you. But the other thing is, once there *is* more, we have to make sure that morality prevails. Morality is the key. Last year, we made more and we grew more, but we didn't give you more. All of the increase was kept for ourselves. That was wrong. The same thing happened the year before, and the year before that. We have to convince everyone to accept morality and next year give some of the increase to you.

So we all have to wait. And while we're waiting, we have to be careful. Because we know you. We know there are some who are the violent ones, the ones who *won't* wait. These are the destroyers. Their children are dying, sick—no medicine, no food, nothing on their feet, no place to live, vomiting on the streets. These are the ones who are drunk with rage, with their lust for revenge. We know what they've planned. We've imagined it all a thousand times. We imagine it every single day. That sound at the door—that odd "crack"—the splintering sound—then they break through the lock and run in yelling, pull us up from where we're gathered at the family table, having our meal, pull our old parents out from the bathroom, pull the little ones up from their beds, then they line us all up together in the hall, slap us, kick us, curse us, scream at us, our parents bleeding, our children bleeding, pulling the children's clothes from the closets, the toys from the shelves, ripping the pictures off the walls. What will they do to us? we ask each other. What?—are they giving all the homes to people who now are living in the street?

Then terrible stories—shops torn apart, random killing, the old professor given a new job: cleaning toilets at the railroad station.

It seems impossible—can that possibly have happened? A mob of criminals—or unemployed louts—people who a year ago were starving in slums? Are they going to be running the factories now, the schools, everything, the whole country, the whole world?

We have to prevent it, although the violent ones are everywhere already, teaching the poor that the way things are is not God-given, the world could be run for their benefit. And so we have to set up a special classroom for the poor, to teach the poor some bloody lessons from the past—all the crimes committed by the violent rebels, by the followers of Marx. Shove the lessons of history down their

The Fever

throats. History, history. The crimes. The oppression. The famines. The disasters. Teach the poor that they must never try to seize power for themselves, because the rule of the poor will always be incompetent, and it will always be cruel. The poor are bloodthirsty. Uneducated. They don't have the skills. For their own sake, it must never happen. And they must understand that the dreamers, the idealists, the ones who say that they love the poor, will all become vicious killers in the end, and the ones who claim they can create something better will always end up by creating something worse. The poor must understand these essential lessons, chapters from history. And if they don't understand them, they must all be taken out and shot. Inattention or lack of comprehension cannot be allowed.

And in places where we find that the classroom is avoided, we must warn the poor that even the innocent are going to get hurt. We can't accept violence against the symbols of law, the soldiers, the police. We have to kill the ones who commit those crimes. But if the violence goes on for a long time, then the ones whose older sisters and brothers we've already killed may be so full of rage that they don't fear death. And to control those people, we may have to go farther—cut out their tongues, cut up their faces, force them to watch us torture their parents, watch the soldiers rape their children. It's the only way to control people who don't fear death.

And so we'll teach the poor that yes, yes, we're going to give them things, but *we* will decide how much we'll give, *and* when, because we're not going to give them *everything*.

And now the ugly little book is back at Chapter One, and I read it again, and Chapter Two, and I read it again, and the water bugs still cover the floor, running in the same complicated patterns, but I brush a few aside and lie down among them. I listen to the strange pounding in my ears.

And it's as if a voice like vomit is coming up slowly from my throat. Stop!

Everyone has always been so good to me.

No. Listen. I want to tell you something. You've misinterpreted everything. The old woman who bent down and gave you sugar-covered buns did not love you. You were not loved the way you thought.

The Fever

Of course I still feel an affection for myself—
someone so happy, cute, funny—?—

No, I'm trying to tell you that people hate you.
I'm trying to explain to you about the people who
hate you.

Why do you think that they all love you? And
what do you think they would love about you?
What are you? There's no charm in you, there's
nothing graceful, nothing that yields. You're simply a relentless, unbearable fanatic. Yes, the com-
mando who crawls all night through the mud is
much much less of a fanatic than you. Look at
yourself. Look. You walk so stiffly into your
kitchen each morning, you approach your cup-
board. You open it, and reach for the coffee, the
coffee you expect to find on its shelf. And it has
to be there. And if one morning it isn't there—
oh, the hysteria!—the entire world will have to
pay! At the very thought of the unexpected, the
unexpected deprivation, you begin to twitch, to
panic, to pant. That shortness of breath! Listen
to your voice on the telephone, listen to the tone
that comes into your voice when you talk to one
of your very close friends and you talk about your

life and you use those expressions—"what I need to live on . . ."—"the amount I need just in order to live . . ." Are you cute then? Are you funny then? That hollow tone—"the amount I need . . ." —solemn, quiet, no histrionics—the tone of hysteria, the tone of the fanatic—well, yes—of course—it makes sense. You understand your situation. Without a place to live, without clothes, without money, you would be like them, you would *be* them, you would be what they are— you would be the homeless, you would be the comfortless. So of course, you know it, you will do anything. There are no limits to what you will do. Without the money, your face would become the face of a rat, your hands would be paws— sharp, nimble, ready to scratch, ready to tear.

Sure, sometimes you think about the suffering of the poor— Lying in your bed, you feel a sympathy, you whisper into your pillow some words of hope: Soon you will all have medicine for your children, soon, a home. The heartless world, the heartless people, like my neighbor Jean, will soon give way, and gradual change *will* happen, as it happened in Holland in the nineteenth century.

But during this period of waiting, waiting, this

The Fever

endless waiting for gradual change, one by one they come knocking at your door and they cry out, they beg you for help. And you say, Get them away from me. I can't stand this constant knocking at the door, these people who come with these ridiculous stories, who claim to be my sister, who claim to be my brother, all day long, day after day. And so all of these people are taken away, and they're made to live in places where they're teased, they're played with, they're lectured, mocked, until a few of them begin to rave irrationally and even laugh, viciously, and then their vicious actions fill absolutely everyone with horror. And then each one of these vicious people is taken by the shoulders and held down, and their head is shaved, and they're strapped into a chair, and they're executed, and the one they're being executed for is you, just as it was always you that all those people were talking about so many years ago when they kept on saying, "For our children's sake, we have to do it, we have to set this town on fire, this barn, this hospital, these forests, these animals, this rice, this honey," just as it's still you, because of how much you love those clean white sheets and the music and the dancers and the telephone calls, for whom all those people with radiant faces are being tortured tonight, are dying tonight.

Do you remember that day in school when you were playing with those three other children, and the teacher appeared in the room with four little cakes and gave all of the cakes, all four of the cakes, to that little boy called Arthur, and none to you or your two other friends? Well, at first all four of you were simply stunned. For that first moment, all four of you knew that what had happened was unjust, insane. But then your friend Ella tried to make a little joke, and Arthur got furious and he hit Ella, and then he went into a corner and he ate all the cakes. It was an example of someone getting away with something.

And your life is another example. It's the life of someone who's gotten away with something. And yet your fanaticism is so extreme that you won't let that thought come into your mind.

Certain things cannot be questioned. The coffee *has* to be there on the shelf, and *no* thought may enter your mind if it conflicts with the assumption that you—yes, you—are a decent person. So go ahead, think—think freely—think

The Fever

about anything you like. Think about your health, other people, the ones who treat you badly, think about the complicated ways in which you mistreat yourself, think about the children afflicted with incurable diseases who were interviewed in that magazine. Think of all the things which show that you're decent, which show that those who are like you are decent—your friends, your loved ones, and all those people all over the world, in every country, who remind you of yourself—people of good will who have a little money but believe sincerely in a better life for all. Think of all the things you've done that were kind, think of the kindness of all your intentions. And if something that you did turned out badly, think of the good motive behind the action—smile, nod your head, understand, accept. Don't talk to people who don't think you're decent. Don't read books, don't read articles, by writers who don't think you're decent, who don't think those who are like you are decent. Their writing is based on a false assumption. It's skewed, distorted. Your thought must be founded on truth, the truth that you are a decent person.

Now, a decent person cannot be a person who's

gotten away with something. A decent person cannot have what it's not appropriate for them to
have. And this understanding of yourself gives you
the basis for a view of the world. And so you can
look out at the way the world works, and sure,
there are many many things that of course disturb
you—the situation of your friend Knut, who loves
Wagner, but who's so badly paid by his publishing
house that he can't even afford to go see the operas
he so deeply loves, or all the examples of man's
inhumanity that you see on your television every
single night, like that terrible overseer on that
rubber plantation in southern Malaysia—but still
you can say that the way the world works is fundamentally not unjust, because you've received a
share of things which you know it's appropriate
for you to have. And if it's appropriate for you to
have the share of things which in fact you have,
and it's appropriate for all the people who are like
you all over the world to have the share that they
have, that means that it's not *in*appropriate for all
of the others to have the share which remains.
You know that what you have is what you deserve,
and that means that what they have is what they
deserve. They have what's appropriate for them

The Fever

to have. And you must admit it. The chamber-maid is repulsive, ignorant—it's not inappropriate that she should live in hell, because to you she really seems like a creature from hell. She spends her life wallowing in dirt, doing sickening things, disgusting things. Can you picture her returning at night to a sparkling apartment?—or going out later to a meticulous performance? No—impossible. What would she do with a beautiful hairbrush, a beautiful comb? She wouldn't know how to appreciate them. What would she do with beautiful bath oils, beautiful towels, beautiful soap? Can you imagine her serving her children beautiful dinners, with fat green vegetables, fat red tomatoes? No—it's appropriate for the chamber-maid to go home at night to that particular hallway on that particular street, just as it's appropriate for you and your friends to spend your lives deciding which products you would like to buy and upholding high standards of performance in art. The way the world works is fundamentally not unjust, so the people who want to preserve the world are basically good, and the ones who want to tear it apart, the ones who steal on the street, the thieves, the destroyers, are basically bad. You—because of your intelligent comments on current films and the thoughtful notes you wrote to your mother's aunt, and because of how upset you were when the waiter in that restaurant brought right up to your table the living lobster that he was going to boil in the kitchen for your dinner—have to be defined as the highest and most admirable type of human being, while Juana the follower of Marx, who, out of some desperate devotion to the people she loves, offers up her body to the torturer's knife, can only be defined as the lowest and most reprehensible type, one who deserves the punishment of death.

I'm floating in space, holding on to a thick iron bar. Far below me, there's a forest. Heat rising up. My hands are so wet they can hardly keep their grip on the bar. I'm terrified of falling, but a voice says, Let go of the bar. I hold on tightly, but the voice says, You won't be hurt. You'll fall safely into the beautiful forest.

I let go, drift through space. I keep thinking, I should have landed by now, but I'm still falling. A few twigs scratch my cheeks almost gently as I fall. I fall so slowly. The forest held in a vivid silence.

The Fever

Now the bathroom floor, the candle, flickering. I lift it, I stand up, I walk out of the bathroom.

Now I'm back in the bedroom, leaning against the wall. Put the candle down on a little table. A breeze comes, from the open window. I draw a chair to the window and sit.

In the street, far away, a man cries out. The earth relaxes. The prisoner in the electric chair has suffered and died, and the guards have taken him out to his grave. And yes—there—there's a wash of blue on the dark wall of the sky, a hint of dawn.

It's the coolest hour of the twenty-four. I look out the window, and in the cool breeze I remember I once was a child in a beautiful city, surrounded by hope. And I feel such joy—the coolness of the breeze—I wonder if I could put down for a moment my burden of lies, of lying—just put it right down on the floor beside me. I wonder what that would be like. Just for a single moment, while the breeze blows in, just to put it down, because I feel so joyful, crazy, naked, free, I want no restrictions on me at all.

Dear God, every muscle of my body aches with the effort of constant lying. I'm twisted, contorted—lying from the minute I get up each day till the minute I go to bed, and even when I'm asleep I think I'm lying. I can't stop, because the truth is everywhere, it's in plain sight—

Listen to me, my darling. Just let it happen, just let it happen just for this moment, just for tonight, and then tomorrow we'll go back to lying again, as if it never happened. We'll pretend it never happened. We'll forget that it happened.

All right, go ahead. Go ahead. Say it.

The life I live is irredeemably corrupt. It has no justification. I keep thinking that there's this justification that I've written down somewhere, on some little piece of paper, that I can't remember what's on the piece of paper, but that it's sitting in the drawer of some desk in some room in some place I used to live. But in fact I'll never find that little piece of paper, because there isn't one, it doesn't exist.

There's no piece of paper that justifies what the beggar has and what I have. Standing naked beside the beggar—there's no difference between her and me except a difference in luck. I don't actually deserve to have a thousand times more than the beggar has. I don't deserve to have two crusts of bread more.

And then, this too: My friends and I were never well meaning and kind. The sadists were not compassionate scholars, trying to do their best for humanity. The burning of fields, the burning of children, were not misguided attempts to do good. Cowards who sit in lecture halls or the halls of state denouncing the crimes of the revolutionaries are not as admirable as the farmers and nuns who ran so swiftly into the wind, who ran silently into death. The ones I killed were not the worst people in all those places; in fact, they were the best.

Nothing is changing in the life of the poor. There is no change. Gradual change is not happening. It's not going to happen. It was only something we talked about.

My feeling in my heart a sympathy for the poor does not change the life of the poor. My believing fervently in gradual change does not change the life of the poor. Parents who teach their children good values do not change the life of the poor. Artists who create works of art that inspire sympathy and good values do not change the life of the poor. Citizens inspired by artists and parents to adopt good values and feel sympathy for the poor and vote for sincere politicians who believe fervently in gradual change do not change the life of the poor, because sincere politicians who believe fervently in gradual change do not change the life of the poor.

The chambermaid's condition is not temporary. A life sentence has been passed on her: she's to clean for me and to sleep in filth. Not, she's to clean for me today, and I'm to clean for her tomorrow, or I'm to clean for her next year. Not, she's to sleep in filth tonight, and I'm to sleep in filth tomorrow night, or some other night. No. The sentence says that *she* will serve, and then on the next day *she* will serve, and then *she* will, and *she* will, right up until her death.

But—the strangest thing of all—although the terms of existence of the chambermaid were settled at her birth, the terms of my existence were not settled at mine.

I say, It's not my fault that I was born with a better chance in life than the chambermaid. It's not my fault that I have a little money and she doesn't.

The Fever

But I don't "have" the money the way I "have" two feet. The money's not a part of me, the fact that I have it isn't a fact about me like my coloring or my race. Through a series of events it came to me, but devoting my life to defending my possession of something that came to me is not an inescapable destiny. Keeping the money is just a choice I'm making, a choice I'm making every day. I could perfectly well put an end to the whole elaborate performance. If people are starving, give them food. If I have more than others, share what I have until I have no more than they do. Live simply. Give up everything. Become poor myself.

I've always loved people who enjoy good meals, people who look forward to watching good performances. Of course I have. Everyone I've ever known is one of those people, I've always been one of those people myself. I've always thought that it's so much nicer to love people who are happy. But the funny thing is that everyone might be. I've struggled hard to get what I have. But my struggle has always been against others. In fact, I've been struggling against the ones who are poor, and from the point of view of the ones who are poor, of course I'm the same as my neighbor Jean.

I'm exactly the same, and I'm not on their side.

And that, too, is a choice I'm making. I could change sides. I could decide to fight on the other side. The life of a traitor? Betraying my own people? Walking into danger? Very difficult, but a possible choice. If I could accept hardship, accept discomfort—why not suffering, prison, and even—?—

I blow out the candle and swim across the room toward my beautiful bed. Inside my covers, head on the pillow, I swim toward sleep. Next week, home.

What will be home? My own bed. My night table. And on the table—what? On the table— what?—blood—death—a fragment of bone—a fragment—a piece—of a human brain—a severed hand.— Let everything filthy, everything vile, sit by my bed, where once I had my lamp and clock, books, letters, presents for my birthday, and left over from the presents bright-colored ribbons. Forgive me. Forgive me. I know you forgive me. I'm still falling.

NOTE

This piece was originally written with the idea in mind that it could be per-fomed in homes and apartments, for groups of ten or twelve.

The piece can be performed by a wide range of performers—women, men—older, younger.